G000150950

THE AIREDALE TERRIER

Airedale Terriers are a fine old breed of English sporting dogs dating back about one hundred years which, through its great growth in popularity over the years, has proven its adaptability to its present day position as family pet. For loyalty, courage, companionship and gentleness with children it is certainly second to none. Mrs Irene Hayes splendid guide has been completely revised and updated by Mrs Dot Hanks, thus ensuring its continued usefulness to all owners—actual or potential— of Airedale Terriers.

THE
AIREDALE
TERRIER

IRENE E. HAYES

Revised by

DOT HANKS

FOYLES HANDBOOKS
LONDON

ISBN 0 7071 0634 6

© W. & G. Foyle Ltd. 1960

First published 1960
Reprinted 1978
Revised edition 1980

Line drawings by Leslie Benenson

Published in Great Britain by
W. & G. Foyle Ltd.,
125 Charing Cross Road,
London WC2H 0EB

Photoset and printed in Great Britain by
Photobooks (Bristol) Ltd.

CONTENTS

ILLUSTRATIONS

1

INTRODUCTION

THE AIREDALE Terrier is widely known as the 'King of the Terriers'. To many of us who know and love him he is 'King of all dogs'. He may also be the royal clown, and the regal guard, such is his adaptability.

Full of character, the Airedale is a wonderful companion and guard who may be trained for the gun, loves a rough and tumble

'Can I help?'–your ever helpful Airedale Terrier (Photo: Animals Unlimited)

with the older children or playing gently and quietly with the younger ones. He is equally happy to accompany you on a long walk, or sit quietly by your side near the fire; and he is ever ready to defend you and yours to the death.

Once you have owned, and been owned by, an Airedale Terrier, it is doubtful you'll ever want any other type of dog. He is adaptable to all styles of living—small cottage or large mansion. Unlike many smaller breeds who spend their time jumping from one place to another and getting under your feet, an Airedale given his 'place' in the house will keep it, and if by chance he is lying stretched out on the floor, such is his trust in you that you can step over him without disturbing him or him upsetting you!

If you want a smart dog what can be smarter than a well-trimmed Airedale Terrier who can enjoy strolling with his owner, or galloping through the woods chasing real or imaginary rabbits?

The ideal family pet!

2

HISTORY OF THE BREED

THE BREED originated more than one hundred years ago in Yorkshire, where it was 'manufactured' by men from that sport-loving district who wanted a breed that was full of stamina, courage and loyalty, with sporting instincts, and a strong swimmer. Many different breeds claim to have had a part in its make up; probably the Old English Terrier and the Otterhound have played the biggest parts. There can be little doubt that the terrier must have had a big influence, while the 'houndy' ears which still occasionally appear and the correct weather-resisting double coat both come from the Otterhound.

The breed was first called the 'Waterside' and later the Bingley Terrier, but eventually the name was settled as the Airedale Terrier, no doubt suggested by the River Aire in the district of its origin. From those early days the Airedale Terrier has, like many other

The Airedale Terrier circa 1876 (from a sketch by Arthur Wardle)

breeds, altered considerably and we now have one of the smartest of terriers which has retained the characteristics it was originally bred for. Although an all-round sporting terrier the Airedale Terrier has since proved it is capable of undertaking many other jobs. For example during the 1914–18 War many Airedale Terriers were trained as Army dogs, both as messengers and as guards. Colonel Richardson's Airedales were well-known and often referred to in the first half of this century.

The police in several countries, including Great Britain, Germany and Japan have used, and in some cases are still using Airedale Terriers as police dogs. Airedales have proved adept at other aspects of work as well, including use as gun-dogs—both pointing and retrieving; and in the U.S.A. Airedales have been used in bear hunts and other big game hunting.

The Otterhound–an ancestor of the Airedale Terrier (Photo: Animals Unlimited)

The other sport in which Airedales have proved popular is the show ring. As can be seen from the photographs the breed has altered a great deal since 1876 and it is today a frequent top honours winner at shows. Probably the most famous Airedale in the show ring to date has been Ch. Riverina Tweedsbairn who achieved the ultimate in the show world—Supreme Champion at Cruft's in 1961 as well as Dog of the Year two years in succession.

Add to all this the gentleness, companionship and courage of the breed and it is easy to see why the Airedale Terrier is such a popular family pet.

Champion Riverina Tweedsbairn Cruft's Supreme Champion 1961

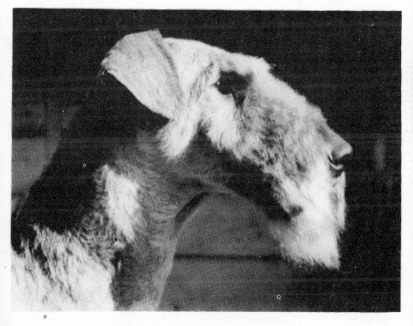

3

THE BREED STANDARD

CHARACTERISTICS Keen of expression, quick of movement, on the tip-toe of expectation at any movement. Character is denoted and shown by the expression of the eyes, and by the carriage of the ears and tail.

General Appearance. The various parts of the dog should be in proportion to each other giving a symmetrical appearance. In movement, the legs should be carried straight forward, the forelegs being perpendicular and parallel with the

Figure 1 Points of the Airedale Terrier

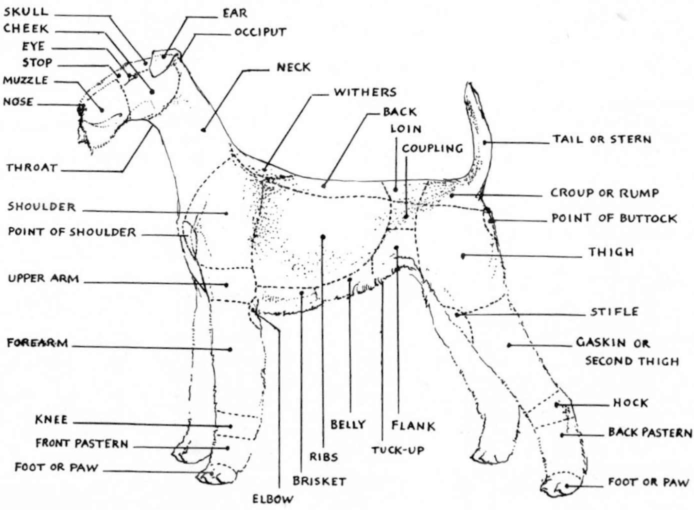

SKULL
CHEEK
EYE
STOP
MUZZLE
NOSE

EAR
OCCIPUT

NECK

WITHERS
BACK
LOIN
COUPLING

TAIL OR STERN

THROAT

SHOULDER
POINT OF SHOULDER

CROUP OR RUMP
POINT OF BUTTOCK

THIGH

UPPER ARM

STIFLE

GASKIN OR
SECOND THIGH

FOREARM

HOCK

KNEE
FRONT PASTERN
FOOT OR PAW

BELLY   FLANK

BACK PASTERN

RIBS   TUCK-UP

BRISKET

FOOT OR PAW

ELBOW

sides. The propulsive power is furnished by the hind legs, perfection of action being found in the Terrier possessing long thighs, and muscular second thighs well bent at the stifles, which admit of a strong forward thrust or snatch of the hocks. When approaching, the forelegs should form a continuation of the straight line of the front, the feet being the same distance apart as the elbows; when stationary it is often difficult to determine whether a dog is slightly out at shoulder, but directly he moves, the defect if it exists, becomes most apparent, the forefeet having a tendency to cross. When, on the contrary, the dog is tied at the shoulder, the tendency of the feet is to move wider apart. When the hocks are turned in (cow-hocks) the stifles and feet are turned outward, resulting in a serious loss of propulsive power. When the hocks are turned outward, the tendency of the hind feet is to cross.

Head and skull. The skull should be long and flat, not too broad between the ears, and narrowing slightly to the eyes. It should be well balanced, with only little apparent difference in length between skull and foreface. The skull to be free from wrinkles, with stop hardly visible, and cheeks level and free from fullness. Foreface must be well filled up before the eyes, not dish-

Figure 2 Conformation showing normal front and rear

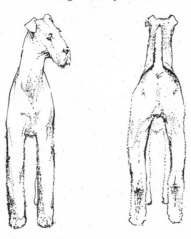

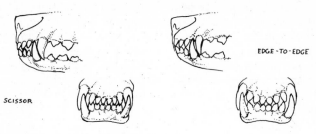

Figure 3 Edge-to-edge and scissor bites

faced or falling away quickly below eyes, but on the other hand a little delicate chiselling should keep appearance from wedginess and plainness. Upper and lower jaws should be deep, powerful, strong and muscular, as strength of foreface is a great desideratum of the Airedale, but there must be no excess development of the jaws to give a rounded or bulging appearance to the cheeks, as 'cheekiness' is not desired. Lips to be tight. The nose should be black.

Eyes. Should be dark in colour, small, not prominent, full of terrier expression, keenness and intelligence.

Ears. Should be 'V' shaped with a side carriage, small, but not out of proportion to the size of the dog. The top line of the folded ear should be above the level of the skull. A pendulous ear, hanging dead by the side of the head like a hound's, is a fault.

Mouth. Teeth strong and level being capable of closing together like a vice.

Neck. Should be clean, muscular, of moderate length and thickness, gradually widening towards the shoulders, and free from throatiness.

Forequarters. Shoulders should be long, well laid back, and sloping obliquely into the back, shoulder blades flat. Forelegs should be perfectly straight, with plenty of bone. Elbows should be perpendicular to the body, working free of the sides.

Body. Back should be short, strong, straight and level, with no appearance of slackness. Loins muscular. Ribs well sprung. In a well ribbed-up or short-coupled dog there is little space between ribs and hips. When the dog is long in couplings some slackness will be shown here. Chest to be deep but not broad.

Hindquarters. Should be long and muscular with no droop. Thighs long and powerful with muscular second thigh, stifles well bent, not turned either in or out. Hocks well let down, parallel with each other when viewed from behind.

Feet. Should be small, round and compact, with a good depth of pad, well cushioned, and the toes moderately arched, not turned either in or out.

Tail. Should be set on high and carried gaily, but not curled over the back. It should be of good strength and substance, and of fair length.

Coat. Should be hard, dense and wiry, and not too long as to appear ragged. It should also lie straight and close, covering the body and legs; the outer coat of hard, wiry, stiff hairs, the undercoat should be a shorter growth of softer hair. Some of the hardest coats are crinkling or just slightly waved; a curly coat is objectionable.

Colour. The head and ears, with the exception of dark markings on each side of the skull, should be tan, the ears being of a darker shade than the rest. The legs up to the thighs and elbows also should be tan. The body to be black or dark grizzle.

Weight and size. Height about 23 inches to 24 inches for dogs, taken from top of shoulder, and bitches about 22 inches to 23 inches. Weight to be commensurate with height and type.

4

PURCHASING YOUR PUPPY

HAVING decided that you want to share your home and your life with an Airedale don't be in too great a hurry to buy one.

Consider first of all whether you want your dog as a pet, or whether the show world might attract you. In either case you should familiarize yourself with the breed standard (see Chapter 3), and try to see as many Airedales as possible. If possible, visit some dog shows where Airedales are scheduled and talk to owners and breeders.

Where to buy a puppy?

Whenever possible it is advisable to buy your puppy direct from the breeder. This way you will be able to see the mother, and will be able to receive advice on diet and the puppy's routine. You should be dealing with someone who is genuinely interested in the breed and wants to see the stock that they have bred well cared for and doing well.

If you are unable to locate a local breeder the Kennel Club will be pleased to put you in contact with one of the Breed Club secretaries (see App. I) most of whom maintain lists of breeders with stock available. Breed Club secretaries are only too willing to help anyone interested in the breed with information and advice. It is often useful to join your local Breed Club who may organize social events where you will be able to meet many people interested in the breed.

Prices for well-reared puppies vary from time to time, and the best way of ascertaining a fair price is, again, to refer to your local Breed Club secretary.

Remember though, pedigree dogs are not cheap to buy, and if they are then be suspicious about how they have been raised.

Dog or bitch?

Having decided where to purchase, the next decision is male or female? As with all things there are advantages and disadvantages with each. Dogs tend to be bigger and may seem more boisterous, though are usually regarded as better house/guard dogs. Bitches may be gentler and more home-loving.

If you decide to buy a bitch remember that she will be 'in season' (on heat) approximately every six months, lasting for about three weeks. This is when she will be most attractive to dogs, and can be mated. If you do not want to show your bitch, or breed from her, it is possible to have the ovaries removed (spayed)—a fairly simple operation usually performed after the first season when the bitch is nine months to a year old. Many people say that spayed bitches grow fat—any dog or bitch will grow fat if overfed and/or underexercised. So if you decide to have your bitch spayed watch her diet and exercise and she should retain her waistline.

Dogs on the other hand have sexual urges all their lives at any time, and unless checked firmly when young their habit for satisfying their urges may become embarrassing and distressing. However, as with all things dogs can be taught what is and is not acceptable.

How old should a puppy be when purchased?

If you want a young puppy it must be at least eight weeks before it leaves its mother. Many breeders may prefer to keep puppies until they are ten weeks old. Never consider buying a puppy under eight weeks of age.

However, if you prefer an older Airedale, say a puppy of six months or a young adult, some breeders occasionally have these for sale, and your Breed Club secretary may well be able to put you in touch with someone.

What to look for when choosing your puppy?

In many cases puppies choose their owners rather than owners choosing them. Watch the puppies playing, see whether one puppy attracts your attention more than the others.

Look for the puppy that comes to meet you, who is prepared to play with you, rather than feeling sorry for the puppy sitting alone who backs away from you.

Healthy puppies should look sturdy and feel firm. Check that the fat tummy is not flabby and bloated (a possible sign of worms).

The eyes should be clear and bright with no sign of discharge or inflammation. There should be no mucous discharge from the nose which should be black. Look into the puppy's ears—these should be clean, free from wax and dirt, and should have no smell about them.

An Airedale puppy often has a fluffy coat; look at the skin under the coat—it should be pink and clear of raw patches, bare patches, or spots of any kind.

Remember the breed standard and look for the sturdy puppy, with a short back and rounded ribs, straight well-boned front legs and small well-padded feet. Look for a long head, with small dark eyes, small neat V-shaped ears and a skull that is free from coarseness. The tail should be set on high, and carried gaily but not curving over the back. Try to visualize your puppy growing up and select the one which will be as near as possible to the standard, and to dogs that you have seen winning at shows.

Check whether the puppy has been wormed—young puppies should be wormed at least twice by the time they are eight weeks old.

When you buy your puppy try to arrange with the breeder that your Veterinary Surgeon will examine the puppy within twenty-four hours and that you may return it if it is not given a clean bill of health. If you have any doubts about the puppy, if there are skin problems, eye discharge or any other health problems then don't buy a puppy from that litter.

Kennel Club Registration

Systems for registering puppies may change from time to time so it may be worth checking with the Kennel Club on the current system.

Enquire whether the puppy is registered with the Kennel Club and make sure that you receive the pedigree form, together with Kennel Club registration and transfer forms if registered.

If you intend to show your Airedale then check that you know the procedure for registering a show dog, and make sure that both the puppy's parents are registered.

When you go to visit the breeder of your puppy make sure that you take all the family who will live with the dog—many breeders prefer to see how many children there are and how they behave with dogs. Remember that buying a dog is a two-way transaction —it's no use buying a puppy and saying that the child left at home because he doesn't like dogs will get used to it—that attitude is not fair to the puppy, or to the breeder, if you have to return the dog after a day or two because someone can't cope.

Finally before collecting your puppy make sure that all your fences and gates are puppy-proof, and that all gate and door catches are secure. Puppies are very inquisitive and can get through very small spaces. A few pounds spent on fencing and catches beforehand may save a lot of heartache later.

So remember—don't be in too great a hurry; look round a little before finally choosing your puppy. He'll be around for a long time so make sure that you make the right decision.

5

PUPPY REARING

THE MAGIC day when you go to collect your puppy arrives. Take some newspaper and old towels with you just in case he's car-sick on the way home.

When you get home let him explore his new surroundings without too much interference and fuss, and introduce him to his bed area. This should be somewhere warm and draught proof—the ideal bed for a young puppy is a large cardboard box with layers of newspaper in it (so that it doesn't matter if he tears it up). It is advisable while he is young to confine him at night and while you are out to an area with an easy-to-clean floor (in many homes this may be the kitchen).

If you have decided that he is to live in a kennel make sure that it is rain and draught proof—dogs can stand the cold, but damp and draughts will kill very quickly. Again, newspaper makes very good, warm bedding in a kennel.

House training

Dogs are creatures of habit, and are usually fairly easy to house-train, provided that you are consistent with a routine and with commands, and are watchful of your puppy. As soon as he wakes up in the morning, or after a nap during the day, put him in the garden and watch until he relieves himself. As soon as he has done this *praise* him and fuss him, let him know that he's done right. Similarly when he's finished a meal put him into the garden and watch until he's relieved himself and fuss him when he has. It's no good putting him out and then going indoors and hoping he will do something, unless you're certain you can't praise him, for unless he knows that something is right he won't learn.

As with all babies he's going to make mistakes indoors. If he does make a puddle or mess indoors, provided you are there when he does it, scold him and immediately put him outside. Don't

21

worry about rubbing his nose in it—all that does is rub it into the carpet and give him a sore nose. If he's confined when you're out, and at night, it is easy to cover the floor with newspapers—it makes clearing up any mess much easier, and after a short while you will find that you don't need to do this. A few weeks of watchfulness, and praise when he does do right, and your puppy will soon learn how to please you.

Similarly other habits about the house are learned through repetition and praise. For example, you probably don't want him jumping all over the furniture and a sharp command 'off' and removal gently to the floor—provided that you are consistent and don't keep changing your mind and picking him up onto your lap for a cuddle—and he'll soon learn that the floor is his place and the furniture is yours.

Inoculation

Remember that your puppy shouldn't be taken into the streets before he has been inoculated against distemper, hardpad and hepatitis. There are two injections, one at ten-twelve weeks of age, and the second two weeks later. Your puppy should not go out until two weeks after the second injection. These diseases are killers and spread very quickly; they are picked up by dogs sniffing where infected dogs have been.

Once inoculated, boosters are given at regular intervals to maintain immunity.

Lead training

While your puppy is confined to the house and garden there is no reason why he shouldn't get used to the collar and lead. Use a light-weight puppy collar and lead, and first of all put the collar only on for about ten minutes. He'll probably spend most of this time trying to scratch it off, but will soon be playing happily with it on, having forgotten that it's there. When he is used to the collar, put the lead on and just let him go where he likes in the garden, leading you. After a short time, try to persuade him to go where you want to go. Short lessons with lots of fuss, and praise, are always more successful than trying for too long and losing your temper—and ending up with a scared dog.

Car training

Just because he can't walk on the pavement or mix with outside dogs doesn't mean he can't be taken for short car rides to get used to the car, or be carried out to see the world with its people, bustle and noise. This will probably overwhelm a young puppy at first, but with lots of fuss and cuddles with humans he trusts he'll soon get used to it.

Feeding your puppy

An Airedale puppy must have enough to eat as it grows very quickly. When you collect your puppy ask if the breeder has a diet sheet and ask for some guidance about the amount of food given. This may vary from puppy to puppy but as a rough guide an eight-week-old puppy should be having four meals a day, two with meat and biscuit meal, and two of milk and cereal.

Appendix II gives a suggested diet chart.

Do not feed your puppy any bones from chicken, lamb or pork as these may splinter. The only bones that are permissible are beef marrow bones.

Many people feel that raw meat is the only thing a dog should be fed on. This is fine if you own a butcher's shop or a slaughterhouse, but for many people raw meat is too expensive. There are many other types of food which suit dogs equally well. What you feed your dog should suit him and you. There are many proprietary brands of tinned and frozen meats, and 'complete' feeds all of which are perfectly good diets for dogs.

If possible stick to what the puppy has been raised on, and if you must change his diet then introduce new food over a period of time so that you do not upset your puppy's tummy.

Make sure that there is always clean water available for your puppy.

Teething

All puppies lose their baby teeth, usually after the age of twelve weeks. During this teething period they may want to chew and bite more than before so it is advisable to provide a large marrow bone (no other bones should ever be given to dogs), or to have one or two chewable toys that won't cause internal problems if lumps are swallowed. It may help your puppy to get rid of loose teeth if you have a tug of war with him using, for example, an old sock filled with rags, or a heavy rubber toy.

When the adult teeth start to come through check that all the baby teeth are out. If two sets of teeth start to grow together this could be painful for your puppy. Remember how uncomfortable you are with toothache, and how fretful babies are when teething. If your puppy seems to be having problems then take expert advice from your Veterinary Surgeon. Most puppies however, lose their puppy teeth and grow their adult ones without their owners even realizing that it's happening.

Grooming

Get your puppy used to being brushed and combed. Spend some time every day standing him for this, preferably using a table or box, and make sure that you comb through thoroughly. Look at his teeth every day. The time you spend doing this now will make your life, and his, much more pleasant when he's older and needs to stand to be stripped, and to be examined by the Vet without fidgeting.

Worming

As I said earlier, when you buy your puppy at eight weeks he should have been wormed at least twice. However, it is likely that you may still see some signs of worms. These signs may be a very bloated, or flabby tummy, a voracious appetite but with little or no gain in weight, loss of condition, or you may see worms in the faeces.

If you think your dog has worms then ask your Vet to prescribe something as there are different types of worms which need different preparations although usually puppies have round-worms.

Rest and exercise

Young puppies get all the exercise they need by playing. DO NOT take young puppies out for long walks.

Rest is very important to all babies and puppies are no exception from this. You will probably find that your puppy will want to sleep after a short play session. Please let him sleep when he wants to. Don't let children pull him around or force him to play when he's tired because that is almost certain to cause a bad-tempered dog. Just think how you feel if you're not allowed to rest or sleep.

Remember, dogs learn by repetition and good habits have to be taught. This includes cleanliness, feeding, grooming and acceptable behaviour. If your dog has bad habits it may be your fault for not being consistent and insisting on the appropriate behaviour. All dogs basically want to please their humans, so if he does right then make a fuss of him—he'll soon learn.

6

GROOMING, TRIMMING AND TRAINING

THE AIREDALE Terrier, like many terrier breeds, does not moult, and can only shed dead hair through regular brushing, combing and trimming.

Your dog should be accustomed to grooming right from the time you collect him and should learn to stand still.

The tools you will need are as follows:

A comb with two-width teeth
A brush with firm bristles
A pair of sharp scissors.

Equipment necessary for your Airedale Terrier (Photo: Anne Cumbers)

Try to use a routine for grooming so that your dog knows what to expect. First of all, stand the dog and comb through with a broad-tooth comb, right down to the skin and being firm about doing all round and below the tail. Comb his belly and always check the feet for lumps of mud and matted hair.

Then comb the back coat with the fine-tooth comb to remove more dead hair.

Make sure that there are no tangles left around the elbows, on the inside of the front and back legs, and under his tummy. When you're sure that the coat is clear of matts and tangles then use a stiff brush—not too stiff so that the skin is scratched—and firmly brush the coat. This stimulates the coat and skin.

The more used your dog is to being handled the easier it will become to groom him—another good habit that can be taught.

Stripping or trimming

As stated the Airedale Terrier does not moult and therefore the coat needs regular stripping to remove dead hair two or three times a year. It is possible that your puppy's breeder may be prepared to do this for you. Alternatively your Breed Club secretary can put you in touch with someone in your area who offers this service. However, the ideal person to strip your dog is *you*. Certainly if you decide to show your dog you will need to do this.

The art of stripping can be learnt—but don't be deceived into thinking it is easy because frankly it is not. Many breeders are happy to give a few lessons, some Breed Clubs run trimming demonstrations and lessons, so it's worth contacting your club secretary to see if anything is organized.

Once you have mastered the skill of using the tools you will get a great deal of pleasure from learning, and have the satisfaction of seeing your Airedale looking really smart.

The tools you need to strip your dog are as follows:
1. A brush and comb.
2. A stripping knife—various sizes and types are available—with a serrated edge, not with a razor blade.
3. A pair of sharp scissors.

The stripping knife is used to remove the dead hairs. Hold the handle in the palm of the hand with the end at the heel of the hand

and the first finger round the shank. Take a few hairs at a time and bring the blade up to the thumb to remove the hair. Always use the knife in the direction of growth of the hair to be removed.

Figure 4 Airedale Terrier trimming chart

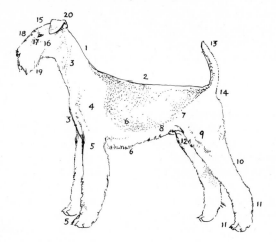

The hair is left at varying lengths on different parts of the body. Figure 4 is a trimming chart giving details of where the hair is trimmed.

1. Trim closely and evenly down into back.
2. Trim back level but not as closely as the neck.
3. Front part of neck and brisket to be trimmed very closely with just a shade more hair left on as one works down to where the front legs join the body.
4. The shoulders to be trimmed evenly and closely.
5. The front legs should be merely trimmed to straightness. Trim principally from rear line. Take out a few hairs from the front and outside of the front legs where they join the shoulder to give a straight line from the top of the shoulder to the feet and from the brisket to the tips of the toes.

6. Shape ribs to follow the body conformation, working hair evenly from a closely trimmed back to a fairly heavy coat on the underpart of the ribs and chest. On the underpart of the chest only remove those hairs necessary to prevent shagginess. Trim under line of chest to follow the body line.

7. Take out loin closer than chest but not too fine. The under line is trimmed closely to emphasize tuck up.

8. Do not take all the hair off the belly but only those that are snarled or shaggy.

9. In this area trim from a fine back to a fairly heavily coated thigh.

10. From middle of thigh to hock trim only those hairs that are shaggy.

11. Trim back line of hock straight. Trim superfluous hairs from edges of feet and between toes. Shape to roundness.

12. Trim insides of back legs clean, taking care to give a clean, even line to the hind legs from the rear view.

13. Trim tail closely to the tip towards the head, take out very fine in rear where it joins the stern.

14. Trim stern very closely where it is joined by the tail, working it heavier toward the hind legs.

15. Trim skull very closely. Trim eyebrows evenly and closely at the outside corner of the eye with plenty of length over inside corner.

16. Trim cheeks closely from outside corner of eye to the corner of mouth.

17. Trim very slightly from inside corner of eye downward to corner of mouth to give proper expression.

18. Trim hairs on top of muzzle from slightly between eyebrows to nose to give straight line from top of skull.

19. Leave chin whiskers, brush forward but clean under jaw from corner of mouth back to neck.

20. Clean off ears closely inside and out, giving particular attention to edges of ear.

Opposite: Great care is necessary when clipping the nails (Photo: Anne Cumbers)

Care of feet

When grooming your dog make a point of inspecting his feet at least once a week. You may find that it will be necessary to keep nails trimmed.

Nails allowed to grow too long beyond the quick become brittle and may break or tear off, and may affect your dog's walking.

Two tools may be used to shorten nails. The nail clipper (see photograph) can be tricky the first few times. Great care is needed not to cut too far back for the quick, if cut, bleeds profusely. When clipping cut a little at a time and look carefully at the area just cut; the nearer the quick the more spongy the underside of the nail becomes. It is often advisable just to clip off any hook on the nail, or just a little then use a coarse file to smooth the rough edges. Always file from the top of the nail downwards.

Figure 5 shows the difference between untrimmed and trimmed nails. Figure 2(A) is the average nail before cutting, showing the extension of the nail beyond the quick. Figure 2(B) shows how closely the nail should be cut to the quick. If the nail is left like this it will wear down evenly in a few days. Figure 2(C) is the nail after filing, with just a thin layer of protecting shell left to shield the tender quick.

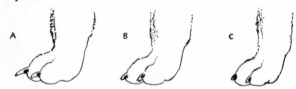

Figure 5 Filing and clipping the nails

Exercise

Now that your dog is more mature he requires regular exercise. The amount must be your decision, but remember that the Airedale Terrier is an active dog and is best kept fit by a sensible diet and regular exercise.

Remember also that if you allow your dog to run free and out of

Opposite: The wrong way of using a check chain (Photo: Anne Cumbers)

control you may be held responsible in law for any damage he causes. So don't let him run free near roads, where he may cause an accident, or near sheep, cattle or any other livestock; and train him always to come back when you call him.

Insurance

Some insurance companies offer third party insurance to cover possible accidents for a low premium, but with a well-trained dog no claims should be necessary.

An obedient Airedale Terrier

As previously written, good behaviour by a dog can be learned by repetition and a great deal of patience on your part. You should by now have instilled in your dog the correct behaviour indoors. However, to be an 'ideal' pet he now needs to learn some other social behaviour, such as walking on the lead without pulling, sitting on command, coming when called and going down when told. As with all training the greatest aid is your patience and consistency of commands. Keep lessons short and keep your temper at all times—a great deal of hard work may be undone by 30 seconds' bad temper.

For training you will need a check collar (or choke chain) and a lead approximately 3 ft long. The check collar must be the correct size for your dog, about 4in longer than your dog's neck size, and it must be used correctly otherwise it may cause distress to your dog. If you are uncertain about the size go to a reputable pet shop who should be able to advise you on the size and the correct method of use.

Walking to heel The aim is to get your dog walking with his head close to your left knee, without any pulling. It is traditional for the dog to walk on the left hand side.

With the lead in the right hand, across the front of you to the dog on your left hand side. Walk off briskly giving the command Heel. Talk to the dog and praise him for staying in the required position. If he pulls in front or to the side a sharp jerk back to the Heel

Opposite: The right way of using a check chain (Photo: Anne Cumbers)

position and more praise when he is there. When giving the sharp jerk the check chain will tighten and make a sharp noise and the two together with your command of Heel will bring him back to you. The check chain if fitted correctly will slacken off while the dog is walking calmly to heel.

Sit With your dog standing at your left hand side, hold the lead in your right hand (shorten it by folding into two), give the command Sit and at the same time raise the lead in your right hand and press his bottom down with your left hand. When he is in the sitting position give him lots of praise whilst keeping him in the Sit.

Down Again with your dog at your left hand side either standing or sitting, take the lead in your right hand, place your left hand across the dog's shoulders, give the command Down and simultaneously press down with the left hand and give a sharp jerk downwards with the lead. Again, as soon as the dog is in the required position make a fuss of him.

Stay A useful extension of the Sit and Down position is to teach your dog to stay where and when told. With the dog on the lead in the Sit or the Down give the command Stay and move two to three paces away. If he attempts to move correct him with a sharp command Stay and make sure that he is in the position you left him. The distance can be extended as your dog learns to stay.

Coming when called It is difficult sometimes to attract your dog's attention when he's off the lead and distracted by nice smells and other dogs. So this exercise should be taught before he is let off the lead.

When you take him out take a very long lead, or a length of rope. Attach to the check collar and allow him to roam at will. When he is not attending to you call his name and the command Come; if he does not respond immediately jerk the line and bring him to you all the time telling him to come. As soon as he reaches you make a fuss of him. Repeat this exercise until he comes as soon as you call. You can then try off the lead. If he does not come immediately keep calling him and *never never* tell him off when he does return. Always make a fuss of him no matter how long it takes you to get

Opposite: Walking to heel (Photo: Anne Cumbers)

him back. If he does not obey you then return to the long line for another spell of training.

There are many excellent dog-training classes where you can learn to train your dog. The Kennel Club or your local Vet should be able to put you in touch with them.

Many people think that training a dog is a knack. Like so many other skills however it can be learnt—the secret is patience, praise, encouragement and persistence. So keep trying without losing your temper, using the same command and same sequence until your dog has learnt how to please you.

Opposite: In the sit (Photo: Anne Cumbers)

7

BREEDING

To breed or not to breed, that is the question!

Give very careful thought to it. Breeding dogs is not a quick easy way of making a fortune; it entails a great deal of hard work and should only be considered if you have suitable facilities to deal with a litter of lively pups.

Many people believe that a bitch should have a litter 'for the sake of her health', or 'to make her live longer', or 'to stop phantom pregnancies'. Having a litter of pups is unlikely to do any of those things. Careful diet, exercise and good care are more likely to provide you with a healthy, happy pet.

Similarly if you have a dog don't be tempted to use him at stud unless you can guarantee a regular supply of bitches. If you can't do this he will find other ways of fulfilling his awakened sexual urges which may not be socially acceptable. Stud dogs are usually only in regular demand if they are shown and are winning regularly, or if they have bloodlines which are very desirable.

Choosing a stud dog

If you wish to breed good Airedales (or any other breed for that matter) considerable thought should be given to the selection of the right stud dog for your bitch.

Don't be afraid to ask for advice from the breeder of your bitch, from the Breed Club secretaries, or from any of the well known, established kennels.

However, generally speaking, if advice is not available, you should study your bitch's pedigree and try to arrange to mate her to a dog whose pedigree contains common ancestors and is therefore related to your bitch. Avoid the temptation to use 'the dog down the road', or go to the nearest dog because it is convenient for the bloodlines may not be linked, and you may not get the results you desire.

When to breed

Most Airedale bitches come into season for the first time between ten and eighteen months of age, and it is not usually advisable to mate a bitch on her first season.

The season lasts for about three weeks and is easily observed by a red discharge and the swelling of the vulva. The best time for mating is some time between the tenth and sixteenth day, usually about the twelfth day.

You should contact the owner of the intended stud dog on the first day of her season to ensure that the dog is available, the charge for use of the dog, and to arrange a date for you to take the bitch for mating. Don't forget that having been mated it is still important that your bitch should have no opportunity of getting with another dog until her season is quite over.

For the first few weeks after mating there is no need to alter the usual routine. The first sign by which you can tell she is in whelp is generally that her teats will be more pronounced, and gradually she will begin to have a heavy, full look. It is often quite impossible to say with certainty that a bitch is in whelp even at six weeks, but it is as well to suppose that she is and act accordingly, as the proportion of bitches that miss is very small.

In order to ensure puppies with good bone add either a proprietary brand of calcium additive to her food, or add sterilized bonemeal, each day, and give either cod liver or halibut oil two or three times a week after the third week of pregnancy. After the first four or five weeks increase her supply of meat daily and as she gets heavier give her rather smaller quantities of food at a time but more often during the day. The extra meat, and milk in addition to her usual quantity of food are quite sufficient.

Normally a bitch has her puppies sixty-three days after mating, but, here again, bitches vary—some have them several days earlier and some two or three days later. I would recommend that your Veterinary Surgeon is told that you are expecting a litter and then, you will find that if you should be in any trouble, even in the middle of the night, he will be ready to help. On the whole Airedales are good whelpers, and need little assistance, but there is always the exception. Ask your Vet to look at her if she goes a couple of days over the usual sixty-three days.

Decide in good time where you wish her to have her puppies and provide her with a good whelping box (see Figure 6). Clean newspaper makes a good bedding, it is easy to obtain, has the advantage of being easily changed each day, and as the time gets near for puppies she will probably tear it into small pieces and make a nest with it. It is a good idea to let her sleep in the box every night for at least two weeks before the puppies are due, and preferably in a quiet place where she will not be disturbed when the time comes.

Once a bitch has started to whelp, careful watch should be kept, but let it be by one person who she trusts. Do not fuss her, treat her calmly and quietly. Some bitches do tend to like their owner with them—to hold their hand!—but others definitely prefer you to interfere as little as possible, and here one must learn as one goes along.

Be prepared with hot water bottles and old towels just in case they are wanted.

There are many excellent books on the subject of breeding dogs, for example 'Dogs and How to Breed them' by Hilary Harmar published by John Gifford, which go into full details of how puppies are born, but briefly each puppy is born in its own little 'bag' and normally comes head first. Sometimes, however, there is a 'breech' birth with the hind legs first. Generally with Airedales little or no assistance is required, but if it is at all possible for you to be present at some other whelping—no matter what breed—

Figure 6 Whelping box

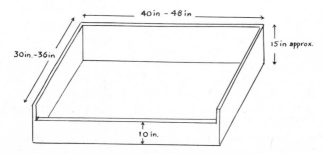

before you start breeding yourself, it would, of course give you more confidence.

An afterbirth comes with each puppy, and the bitch will generally clear everything up after each one is born. If however, your bitch makes no attempt to deal with the puppies you must open the bag, making sure that you have well scrubbed your hands beforehand, and break the cord about three inches from the puppy. Dry the puppy and place with the bitch to allow it to feed before the arrival of the next puppy.

If the bitch seems to resent any interference at all, leave her alone—just keep a careful watch that all is well. Usually, this type of bitch is the best whelper of all—gets on with the job well and quickly and makes one realize how wonderful Nature can be.

If the bitch starts to strain and does not produce a puppy within about two hours then is the time to ask for help. It is most cruel to leave a bitch with no assistance and may result in the loss of the bitch and the puppies.

It is as well to ask your Vet to call within twenty-four hours of your puppies being born to ensure that all is well, to give Mum an antibiotic injection to deter any infections and to ensure that nothing has been retained in the womb.

Don't worry about white toes, or small white marks on the chest as these will probably grow out in a few weeks, but look for any deformities in the puppies such as cleft plate. If there are any deformed puppies, or very weak puppies it will be kinder to let your Vet put them to sleep rather than to try to raise them.

Care of the brood bitch and her puppies

Once the puppies have safely arrived and the bitch is clean and comfortable with her family, give her a warm drink and keep her as quiet and undisturbed as possible. For at least the first twenty-four hours keep the bitch on a light diet and after that time give her plenty of meat which will help to increase her milk supply. To her usual diet, with extra meat and milk drinks, continue to add the calcium or bonemeal and the cod liver or halibut oil. It will require at least four meals a day to ensure that your bitch does not get too pulled down by her family.

It is important to see that the bitch and puppies are kept warm.

Not a problem in the summer, but in the winter it may be necessary to introduce some artificial heat into the whelping area to maintain the right temperature for the puppies for at least the first week.

When the puppies are about three–four days old they must have their tails docked and dew claws removed. Either ask your Vet to do this for you or another experienced breeder. Ensure that the tails are not docked too short. Approximately one-third of the tail is removed, and it is better for a tail to be left a little too long rather than too short.

As puppies grow so do their nails; to keep Mum comfortable it is essential to keep the tips trimmed otherwise the bitch's teats and tummy could be scratched and may make her sore and bad tempered.

As the puppies get older the bitch will spend less time with them, and you should start weaning them onto solid foods between three and four weeks of age. Start by offering each puppy a small amount of a baby Cereal (e.g. Farex) with milk. They will soon learn to lap this up. After a day or two try each puppy with a couple of teaspoons of very finely minced meat. They may be a bit slow for a few days, but they will quickly learn and should shortly be on two meat meals and two milk and cereal meals each day, plus whatever Mum can still supply.

It's amazing how quickly puppies grow and, of course, the amounts you feed will need to be increased fairly rapidly to allow the puppies sufficient food. Watch them feeding and make sure that the slower feeders get their fair share, if necessary separate the slower feeders from the greedy puppies whilst they are feeding.

Weaning should be completed by the time the puppies are six to seven weeks old. It is essential to ensure that the puppies receive the necessary vitamins etc., so continue the bonemeal or calcium additive daily and the cod-liver oil twice a week.

Remember to worm your puppies when they are about five weeks old. You can buy proprietary brands of wormer, or your Vet will prescribe something for you. Whatever you use follow the instructions carefully and you should have no trouble. To ensure that the puppies are free from worms when they go to their new homes they should be wormed at least once after the initial dose (usually 10–14 days later), and it may be as well to suggest to purchasers that they worm the puppy again after they have had it for a few weeks.

When selling your puppies remember how you felt when you collected your first puppy, and try to give the purchasers as much assistance as you can, including a diet sheet and some idea of the amount of food being given.

8

SHOWING

Mention dog shows and the name that immediately springs to mind is Cruft's—probably the most famous dog show in the world. To show at Cruft's is many people's ambition, but it is a privilege reserved for those dogs who qualify during the previous year. However, there are dog shows throughout the year—more than 4,000 during the year—in every part of the country, from the largest championship show to the local Canine Society match.

If you decide that you want to show your dog it is worthwhile to visit as many shows as possible before entering, to watch and learn. You'll probably meet a crowd of friendly enthusiastic people enjoying their favourite pastime, who will be happy to talk to you about the skills of Airedale preparation and showing. (Preferably after they have finished showing their dogs).

Details of forthcoming shows are advertised in 'Dog World' and 'Our Dogs' published weekly. Your Breed Club Secretary may also be able to give you details of Airedale Terrier Club shows.

If this is your first attempt at dog showing you may find it helpful to attend a local Ringcraft Class where some of the skills of dog showing are taught. These classes are held in many parts of the country and the Kennel Club should be able to put you in touch with your local club.

When visiting a show watch what happens to the Airedales both in and out of the judging ring. Before judging, exhibitors will be busy preparing their dogs and you can learn a lot by watching what they do, and (after judging) asking questions about the preparation and trimming. When the dogs enter the judging ring the handler will be given a ring number—this tallies with the number in the show catalogue which shows details of the dog and its breeding. The ring number is the only identification that the judge will have of that dog. When all the dogs have gathered the judge

47

may ask them to move round the ring, or alternatively he may begin the individual examination of each dog.

This entails the judge looking at the dog's eyes and his teeth (to check that the bite is correct). He will feel the coat texture and run his hands over the dog to feel the bone structure. He may also examine the dog's feet. The judge will then allow the dog to pose so that he can get an overall picture of the dog. The handler will be asked to move the dog so that the judge can ascertain that movement is correct.

So before entering for a show your dog must be trained to know what to expect. You should teach him to stand in the show stance. Again watch winning dogs at shows. They stand up on their toes, back legs thrust back in a natural way, and they look keen, alert—on tip toe of expectation. Ask friends to 'go-over' your dog as the judge would, to look at his teeth, to pick up his feet and to run hands over his head, back, legs and tail. If this is done from an early age your dog will find nothing strange about his first show, he'll know what to expect and be confident to face

Ch. Perrancourt Playful top Airedale Terrier in 1978 and 1979 and top dog for all breeds in the U.K. 1979 (Photo: McFarlane)

Proud mum with litter.

Puppies at three weeks.

"Now I'm older I like exploring".

One way to travel in comfort.

HGM 865N

Dog being examined by a judge.

"Is it our turn yet?"

"I thought I'd sit in the garden for a while

Colour photos by Anne Cumbers

"Then I thought - why sit when I can relax properly.

it. A dog who knows what is expected of him and has been taught how to behave will have a distinct advantage over those who will not show off their best points. Teach your dog to move both in a circle and a straight line on a loose lead without pulling—as you will see the judge requires the dogs to move. Remember—it's the dog that the judge wants to see moving NOT YOU, so always keep your dog nearest to the judge.

Before showing your dog you will, of course, need to trim him in the accepted style. The trimming chart in Chapter 6 shows the basic routine, and you will find it useful to spend time at shows talking to exhibitors and seeing how the dogs are trimmed and prepared. Some Breed Clubs hold trimming lessons and demonstrations and it may be worth contacting your local Breed Club secretary to see if there are any classes in your area. Trimming an Airedale for showing is a very time-consuming hobby, and the final effect with the correct finish and expression requires much patience and practice.

As with all things practice makes perfect and persistence is essential if you are to succeed.

Entering a show
Having got your dog looking right and trained for the show ring the next step is to enter your first show. There are several different types of show—the biggest being the general championship shows where there may be upwards of 8,000 dogs of all breeds entered from all over the country; the other types of shows being Open Shows, Limited (for members of societies) and Sanction Shows. All these types of shows are licensed by the Kennel Club and run in accordance with Kennel Club Rules and Regulations. Some of the Breed Clubs run shows and a good place to start your show career would be at a Breed Club limited show. Alternatively your local Canine Club may run a limited show for their members. The limited shows are the smallest type of show and usually have a more relaxed atmosphere where you and your dog will be able to do justice to your training.

Having decided where you will try your new skills the first stage is to request a schedule of classes from the Show Secretary. This will show the classes available together with the definitions of

eligibility for entry to the classes. Read the definitions carefully—
you will see that some classes are restricted by the dog's age—for
example PUPPY—for dogs of six and not exceeding twelve
calendar months of age on the day of the show—whereas other
classes are restricted by the amount of winning done by a dog.
Remember that in the classes restricted by age the amount of
winning done by the dog is not taken into account. When beginning
it may be better to enter your dog in the lowest class for which he is
eligible.

The schedule will also show a closing date for receipt of
entries—usually at least two weeks prior to the date of the show;
this is to allow the Show Secretary time to prepare the show
catalogue. Also in the schedule will be an entry form on which all
entries must be made. This form should be completed in block
capitals and the classes you wish to enter shown in numerical
order. You must also sign the entry form and date it (the form will
have an undertaking for you to sign which should be carefully

Ch. Tanworth Merriment top Airedale Terrier 1977 (Photo: Garwood)

read). The entry form and all entry fees should then be sent to the Show Secretary prior to the date of closing of entries.

Remember that before you can enter your dog at a Kennel Club Licensed Show he must be registered with the Kennel Club, and if it has been registered by the breeder you must transfer it to your name. The necessary forms are available from the Kennel Club (for address see Appendix I). You can however enter a show if you have applied for the transfer of registration but have not received notification of completion from the Kennel Club.

There is another type of show that can be a useful training ground for you and your dog. These are the shows held with Kennel Club permission (and include local Canine Society matches for their members). Exemption Dog Shows are held throughout the year, usually in aid of charity; dogs need not be registered to enter and entries are taken on the day of the show. There are usually four classes restricted to pedigree dogs, and a number of novelty classes open to any dogs including crossbreeds. Exemption Shows are great fun and will give you and your dog good experience.

The Airedale Terrier Breed Clubs (listed in Appendix 1) can be most helpful to new Airedale owners and exhibitors, and you may find that the local breed club runs social events, trimming demonstrations and club shows so that you can meet with other Airedale enthusiasts. Breed Club secretaries are always willing to help with advice on Airedale problems or put you in touch with other exhibitors or breeders who may be able to help you.

When you get to your first show find out where and when the Airedales will be judged. Try to remember what you have seen at shows you have visited to watch and learn, and put some of it into practice. You should have got your dog looking his best and knowing what to expect, so when called go confidently and quietly into the ring satisfied that your dog will do his best as you've done yours. Don't forget to make a fuss of your dog after the judging is over, even if you haven't won a prize. Accept the fact gracefully, and fuss your dog so that he associates it all with pleasure—remember 'many men, many minds'—next time you show perhaps you will gain a coveted prize card.

9

HEALTH OF YOUR DOG

As THE proud owner of an Airedale Terrier you will, of course, be concerned that he receives the best treatment and health care. This chapter gives some basic information about the health care of your dog, although a very important person for this will be your Veterinary Surgeon.

When you buy your dog it is worthwhile asking your Vet to give him an examination as soon as possible after purchase so that you know the dog is in good health to start life with you. It is also a good opportunity for your dog to get to know the Vet without having any unpleasant or painful treatment.

Temperature
The normal dog's temperature is 101.5°F. (38.6°C.). The temperature is taken in the rectum.

Any rise in temperature lasting more than one day must be taken seriously and warrants a visit to your Vet.

Care of the teeth
Your dog's teeth should be checked regularly both to ensure that nothing is caught in them, and to make sure there is no damage. This check should form part of the grooming procedure. Dogs who chew hard-baked dog biscuits or large bones usually keep their teeth clean, but if tartar forms and discolours the teeth it may need to be removed by descaling. However, it is possible to clean your dog's teeth regularly either with a brush or a piece of rag and a mixture of salt and baking soda, or toothpaste.

Although bones will help to keep teeth clean they should not be given too frequently as they can cause internal problems. The only bones that may be given are large marrow bones. *Never* give a dog chop bones, chicken, rabbit, lamb or pork bones as these may splinter and cause serious internal injuries to dogs.

Care of ears

Keep the hair trimmed from around and in the ears. Never wash out your dog's ears with soap and water. Clean them with a cotton wool swab dipped either in mild peroxide or olive oil. Never probe deeper in the ear than you can see. If the ears feel unusually hot, seem sore or sensitive, have any discharge or foul smell then a visit to your Vet is essential.

Care of the eyes

Usually the eyes are clear and bright, with no discharge or inflammation. Any unpleasant discharge, or if your dog rubs his eyes, must be dealt with by your Vet.

Sometimes a dog will pick up a foreign body in the eye when exercising in high grass or rough ground. This can be washed out with warm water; however, if the dog seems distressed or the eye inflamed then the Vet should examine it.

Care of the skin

The normal dog's skin should be free of any blemishes, firm and clean. Skin diseases like mange and eczema need expert attention and must be treated by your Vet.

If your dog's skin seems dry and flaky (scurfy) try adding a little cod liver oil to his food twice a week.

Dogs should not be bathed too frequently as this removes much of the natural oils from their coats, but if your Airedale does have to be bathed then use a proprietary brand of dog shampoo (not washing up liquid as this is too strong for their skin) and make sure that all traces of the shampoo are rinsed from the skin and coat. Dry him thoroughly before allowing him to go out of doors. Normally most of the dirt would be removed from the coat in the grooming process.

Giving your dog medicine

Pills—these are usually easier to administer than liquid medicine. They can be disguised in a tit-bit for him and most dogs will take them that way. However, if you want to give a tablet without disguise (for example on an empty stomach) then with the dog sitting in front of you open his mouth — either by firmly pressing the sides of the mouth or by gently inserting fingers into the mouth at the front and pressing down so that the mouth is wide open— then place the tablet as far to the back of the tongue as possible. Close the mouth and support the head so that the nose is pointing into the air and the throat is a straight line and gently stroke the throat until the dog swallows. The tablet should have disappeared with the swallow.

Liquid medicine—this can be tricky particularly if the medicine is sticky or smells unpleasant. Two people can usually achieve better results than one. With the dog in the Sit, have one person standing behind him supporting his head and opening his mouth by pressing gently on the sides of the mouth; when the mouth is open you can then quickly give the medicine and take the mouth upwards, but not quite into the straight line otherwise the dog may choke on the liquid.

When the medicine has successfully been taken make a big fuss of your dog.

Common ailments

Diarrhoea: All dogs suffer from this at some time, and often it can be caused by their diet, as much as by an infection. If your dog is suffering then do not give him anything to eat for 24 hours, if the diarrhoea still persists then you must take him to your Vet. You should also consult your Vet if there are other symptoms such as listlessness, lack of appetite, excessive drinking or a high temperature.

When the diarrhoea clears up then put your dog onto a light diet of well-cooked boiled rice, boiled fish or chicken for a day or two to allow the system to recover.

Constipation: This is often related to diet. Allow your dog fresh vegetables and roughage, give him moistened biscuit meal. Bones given too frequently can cause constipation.

For quick relief give some form of oil such as olive oil, and if the problem persists obviously seek help from your Vet.

Distemper: Thanks to the modern inoculations distemper in its worst form is seldom seen today. However, the word is used in a broader sense to describe a number of symptons. These include high temperature, loss of appetite, diarrhoea, listlessness, vomiting, thick discharge from the nose and eyes. These may also be symptoms of other complaints less serious than distemper.

If your dog should show these symptoms keep him warm, check his temperature and get help from your Vet as soon as you can.

Worms: In the Chapter on puppy rearing the subject of worms is mentioned, but adult dogs can also have worms, and all dogs should be wormed, usually for round worm, at least once a year. There are many different types of worms, such as roundworm, tapeworm, hookworm. Each requires a special treatment, and if you suspect that your dog has worms then your Vet is the right person to treat the dog. He may ask you to take specimen faeces in for examination to determine the type of worm, and will prescribe the appropriate medication. It is usually necessary to give two doses of medication, one ten days after the first.

Symptoms of worms—you may see worms or worm segments in bowel movements, or vomit. The dog may look 'pot-bellied', may have a cough, suffer from diarrhoea, vomiting, and have runny eyes and nose.

Fleas: Even the best dogs suffer occasionally from fleas, and if you do find them on your dog you must tackle not only the dog but also his bedding or kennel. Fleas drop off dogs to lay their eggs and may therefore also be in the carpets, so treatment should include anywhere in the house that the dog visits.

There are a number of proprietary brands of flea powder and aerosols on the market; these should be used in accordance with the instructions on the container. You could also bath the dog but make sure that you get every bit of him wet (put some cotton wool in his ears to stop the water getting in) and wash all over including the top of his head, minding his eyes. It is advisable to do two or three treatments at ten days' intervals to ensure that any eggs hatched are eliminated.

Thoroughly wash all bedding, and spray and vacuum the carpets and furniture. If your dog is kennelled then treat the kennel thoroughly with an appropriate cleaner.

Lice: Lice are much more difficult to dispose of than fleas, and it may be better to seek advice from your Vet if you suspect that your dog has lice.

Ticks: These may be picked up from wild-life such as hedgehogs, or squirrels, or from sheep. They look like grey or pinkish lumps and may be mistaken for warts. The tick buries his head into the dog's skin and should not be pulled off as the head left attached may go septic. They are best removed either by soaking cotton wool in spirit (alcohol, T.C.P. methylated spirit) or by touching the tick with a lighted cigarette—this causes the tick to loosen its grip and it can be plucked off. Grasp the tick as near to the skin as possible, if you pull a bit of skin with it don't worry. When the tick is removed disinfect the spot thoroughly.

Cuts: If your dog cuts himself clean the cut thoroughly, but don't stop him licking it. His tongue will both clean the cut and remove any foreign matter from it. Deep cuts, or those where skin is missing should be treated by your Vet.

Care of the older dog

A great deal of this book has concentrated on your Airedale as a puppy. Puppies develop very quickly into adults and your dog should be a mature dog by the time he is two years old. The average life expectancy of an Airedale is about twelve years, and may be as long as fourteen years.

As he gets old he will begin to take life slower, still enjoying his exercise but needing shorter, quieter walks, without the boisterous romps and play that you both used to enjoy. Make sure that he gets plenty of fresh air, but don't let him get cold. With less exercise he may require a slightly different diet, with less starch and perhaps having two small meals rather than one big meal each day.

Old age makes its mark and as time goes on grey hairs start to show and your dog's faculties may become impaired. However, provided he is still enjoying life, and eating well, then well and good. But, should the infirmities make your pet's life difficult for him and a burden then it is far kinder to ask your Vet to give him sleep without suffering, leaving you with all those happy memories.

APPENDIX I

THE AIREDALE TERRIER BREED CLUBS

THERE are currently eight Airedale Terrier Clubs in the United Kingdom, seven of these are geographically based, and there is one national club.

THE NATIONAL AIREDALE TERRIER ASSOCIATION*
THE AIREDALE TERRIER CLUB OF NORTHERN IRELAND*
THE AIREDALE TERRIER CLUB OF SCOTLAND
THE MIDLAND COUNTIES AIREDALE TERRIER CLUB*
THE NORTHUMBERLAND & DURHAM AIREDALE TERRIER CLUB*
THE NORTH OF ENGLAND AIREDALE TERRIER CLUB*
THE SOUTH OF ENGLAND AIREDALE TERRIER CLUB*
THE WEST OF ENGLAND & SOUTH WALES AIREDALE TERRIER CLUB*

*Denotes those clubs currently organizing Shows, and most of the regional clubs organize some social events for their members.

The Kennel Club will be able to give the name and address of the current Secretary for each of the Clubs. The Kennel Club's address is: 1 Clarges Street, London, W1Y 8AB. Telephone: 01 493 6651

071

0227
752854

APPENDIX II

SPECIMEN DIET SHEET FOR PUPPIES

2 months	Morning	Milk with cereal (Cornflakes, Weetabix, of Farex).
	Mid-day	Meat with biscuit meal. (Spillers Puppy Meal soaked in hot water or Oxo gravy before adding to meat).
	Early evening	Milk with cereal, or occasionally a beaten egg in milk
	Late evening	Meat with biscuit meal
3 months		As above, but with increased quantities
4 months	Morning	Milk with cereal
	Mid-day	Meat with biscuit meal
	Mid–late evening	Meat with biscuit
5/6 months	Morning	Milk with cereal
	Mid–late evening	Meat with biscuit meal
9 months	Evening	Meat with biscuit meal (A coarser grade of biscuit meal can be used from age 4 months)

Fresh water should be available at all times

Quantities are not stated as all dogs require different amounts. To judge this, an adult Airedale will need between 1–1½lbs. of meat a day.

Meat meals can be varied by adding a little raw vegetable (carrot, greens, onion) finely chopped, or by adding an Oxo or some stock gravy to the meal.

Fish can be given as an alternative to meat. Please ensure that all sharp bones are removed.

Some form of calcium should be added to one of the meat meals each day, such as Stress.

INDEX